MW00900128

Book Coming in 2014

"An Introduction to Engaging with the King"

Titles Available in 2013

"An Introduction to the Seven Spirits of God"
"The Spiritual Dynamics of Hand Drumming"
"A Mystical Introduction to Angels"

© Copyright 2014

All rights reserved. This book is protected by the copyright laws of the United States of America. This book may not be copied or reprinted for commercial gain or profit. The use of short quotations or occasional page copying for personal or group study is permitted and encouraged. Permission will be granted upon request. Unless otherwise identified.

Scripture quotations are from the New King James Version ®. Copyright © 1982 by Thomas Nelson, Inc. Used by permission. All rights reserved. Scripture quotations marked AMP are taken from the Amplified ® Bible, Copyright © 1954, 1958, 1962, 1964, 1965, 1987 by the Lockman Foundation. Scriptures marked NIV are taken from the HOLY BIBLE, NEW INTERNATIONAL VERSION®, Copyright 1973, 1978, 1984 International Bible Society. Scriptures marked YLT are taken from Young's Literal Translation of the Holy Bible by Robert Young, Copyright 1862

Emphasis within Scriptures is the author's own.

Extra-biblical references marked Enoch are taken from George W.E. Nickelsburg and James C. VanderKam. *1 Enoch: A New Translation* (Minneapolis: Fortress, 2004).

Table of Contents

Preface

"You call yourself leaders, but your fear-motivation leads you nowhere! By your words and public actions, you don't give permission to others to enter the Kingdom of Heaven and you won't even go in yourselves."

My hope is to never shut the door to the Kingdom to anyone with or without my actions. I desire my entering the Kingdom to be an encouragement, an invitation to all.

> I believe that by constantly believing that Heaven is open;
> You can constantly experience it!

Matthew 13:52 Amplified Bible (AMP)

[52] *He said to them, Therefore every teacher and interpreter of the Sacred Writings who has been instructed about and trained for the kingdom of heaven and has become a disciple is like a householder who brings forth out of his storehouse treasure that is new and [treasure that is] old [the fresh as well as the familiar].*

This book is my attempt to bring substance from my storehouse, some stories, scripture, and experiences, which will encourage you to be a mature citizen of the Heavenly kingdom. We all need to know and interact with those who work among you. We need to be mature & effective in both realms – the seen & unseen.

Introduction

It all begins with desire. But I think in our culture we have made some desires unobtainable. It may be easier if we de-mystify the word "desire" and re-define it as simply as a "non-necessary want". When younger during Christmas season, I would create a list of wants and give it to my Father. It was a list of my Christmas desires.

> ### Luke 12:31-32 (AMP)
> [31] *Only aim at and strive for and seek His kingdom, and all these things shall be supplied to you also.*
> [32] *Do not be seized with alarm and struck with fear, little flock, for it is your Father's good pleasure to give you the kingdom!*

In the summer of 1975, my Father, who was in the US Army, was assigned to Ft. Leavenworth. This was my first time in Kansas: here I would almost drown during swim practice, play my first year of high school football, experience my first crush, and meet my first girlfriend. Kansas would prove to be a place of many unique encounters.

In that Christmas season, our family attended a Sunday church service. After three hymns, the Chaplain called the younger children to the front of the chapel for a story before being dismissed to Sunday school. Since it was the season, he told a Christmas story. I do not recall the story verbatim, but it was the story where the angels announced the good news. The congregation and I watched the gathering and patiently waited for the "better" stories reserved for the sermon. The chaplain finished his story and dismissed the kids to their classes. The kids ran off. But one stopped short of the exit, did an 180° turn and yelled, "Pastor, do I got an angel?" The congregation giggled. With a smirk, the pastor said, "Yes, you do". The kid was satisfied and took off for his cookies and juice.

I don't remember the sermon but I do remember that interaction between the pastor and the boy. Our family drove home for lunch and then waited for the youth meeting. The weekly youth meeting was one of the main things I missed while at college.

Later that night, I attended the regular Sunday night youth meeting. I was dropped off at the youth leader's house by my parents. I was in for more than the normal catching up and seeing friends; I was in for a surprise. The group leader settled us down and made announcement, "Hey everyone, earlier today I got a call, listen to this story: This morning a little boy went home from Sunday school and met his (guardian) angel." The details:

> After church the little boy and his parents went home. They probably ate lunch together. After the meal, some cleanup, the little boy went to his room. While in his room, he met his angel. With great zeal, the boy ran out of his room. He found his parents and described the visitor. After the boy shared his "fantastic" story with mom & dad, they asked one question, "Who said, you had an angel?" The little boy responded, "Pastor did". The dad picked up the phone and called the pastor, "Pastor, I need to see you in your office in 15 minutes. My wife and son will meet you there, click…"
> They sat across the desk from the pastor. The boy shared his story (height, width, color, conversation with the angel …) for the 2nd time. At the end of the story, the parents said, "Well?" The pastor paused, scratched his head, and did other delay tactics. In the pregnant silence, the parents said, "How could he see his angel and we have not seen ours?" The pastor looked up and said, "I'm not sure, but the boy's story sounds valid to me". The little boy smiled. The parents frowned. The family left.
> After they left his office, the pastor picked up the phone and called my youth leader.

That night, I heard my first non-Christmas angel story. I could not wait to get home. I was there that morning at church. I saw the kids in front of the chapel. I saw the little boy. I heard him ask the question. If he could see his angel --- I definitely could see mine.

My parents picked me up from youth group. They asked me how it was. I mumbled. I was busy thinking, "What are the "magic words that make angels appear and how did the little boy know them?"

Finally home, I went down to my basement bedroom. I sat on my waterbed and replayed all the "angel facts" from the day. This can't be too complicated. I dropped to my knees at the foot of my bed. My prayer was something like, "God, that little boy saw his angel – I wanna see mine". I waited. Nothing happened. I stood up and rubbed my sore knees. The basement floor was concrete.

I pondered, "Maybe my prayer was not humble or child-like enough." Back to the knees, I paused and said something like "Father, I know I have an angel. I would like to see mine if possible." I thought, "That was a much better prayer."

I waited. Eyes shut, on my knees – the perfect prayer position – This time I was not disappointed. I could feel something in the room. There was something standing next to me. In that instant, I exchanged my "want" for "fear". I started screaming, "Go Away, Go Away!" I screamed until the feeling went away. I open my eyes and nothing was there. I didn't think it was going to feel like that – I guess I was not ready for "the kingdom".

I didn't learn any magic words but, I did learn and that will be shared in the coming chapters.

New Mystic

P.S. The above story actually finishes (starts again) in thirty-six years.

Chp 1: One Thing

"Problems created with this consciousness can only be resolved from a higher consciousness" – Albert Einstein

On some stage of my journey, I came to realize that my "active" mind was more of a liability than an asset. We live in an age of information. So much information that most of our energy is spent throwing away data that we think is of no value. The other portion of energy is used to separate the distractions from true revelations. So I set out to try to find a way to discipline my very active mind. I needed a means to clarify, focus, so I could effectively pursue. Those words are popular in the business segments of our culture but are also viable in other areas of our life. I believe those areas (clarity & focus) were key to maturing in Yeshua, *"seek His kingdom, and all these things shall be supplied".*

> **Clarity:** being clear about what you really want to achieve

> **Focus:** avoiding distractions and concentrating on higher order information that would lead to activities that produce

I felt a part of maturity was to have these qualities. As I pondered these different attributes, a phrase came to mind, "ONE THING I DESIRE…"

> <u>**Psalm 27:4**</u>
> **"One thing** have **I desire**d of the Lord, that will I seek after; that I may dwell in the house of the Lord all the days of my life, to behold the beauty of the Lord, and to enquire in his temple."

I then realized that I was fairly clear and I was ready to pursue but my "focus" was lacking. It was tough for me to focus on **ONE THING** for any period time. So I thought that meditation might help me focus on the **ONE THING**.

So, I searched the internet for some free guidance on the discipline of meditation. In a previous book, I shared some techniques for meditating and achieving a state, an atmosphere for engaging the Kingdom of our God. As citizens of the Kingdom, we need to be more aware, knowledgeable, and familiar with His domain.

Here are the steps from my first book:

1. Set aside a calm, quiet place (I tried soothing music but it became another distraction)

2. Sit comfortably (note: when I laid down I would sleep, so sit)

3. Slow your breathing

4. Breathe deeply (slow & steady)

5. I would focus on an image in my mind (eyes closed): "An ocean shore with gentle waves lapping my feet then watching the water recede and return"

6. I would try to set my breathing on the wave cycle: breathing in with the wave coming to shore; breathing out as the water receded

7. I would try to stay focused only at the waves for 5 minutes.

It took months before I could get to five uninterrupted minutes. In the beginning, it would take me 30 minutes just to get through the first five steps.

My exercises were designed to increase or build my ability to **focus** and not be so easily distracted. I would follow the steps as often as I could.

While writing this book, I found another benefit of meditating. It seems that our thought life has a role in our participating/engaging in/with the "kingdom of Christ and of God".

> **Ephesians 5:5**
> *"For be sure of this: that no person practicing sexual vice or impurity in thought or in life, or one who is covetous [who has lustful **desire** for the property of others and is greedy for gain]—for he [in effect] is an idolater—has any inheritance in the **kingdom** of Christ and of God.*

According to the above verse, "… no person practicing sexual vice or impurity in **thought…** *has any inheritance in the kingdom of Christ and of God."* Meditating can help focus your thought life. You can be a person practicing the opposite of sexual vice and the opposite of impurity in thought. My meditative goals were designed so I could "hold a thought" – that was good. With that foundation, we can move to the best things. We need the right, correct thoughts. I've found great benefits meditating on my relationship with Abba (Father God).

So, I've updated my meditating steps. I attended a conference in April 2013 that talked about the four faces of God. Meditating on the Father accelerates the metamorphosis into becoming like Him. This transformation is the Fathers goal; it should be ours too. We shall be like Him.

> **2 Corinthians 3:18**
> *"But we all, with unveiled face beholding as in a mirror the glory of the Lord,* **are transformed into the same image** *from glory to glory, even as from the Lord the Spirit."*

So when I make the time, I follow the below regimen:

1. Go to a quiet place

2. Stand

3. I would begin to focus on the name of God, YHVH, by repeating each letter out loud:

    a. A full exhale pronouncing (Y) "Yode",
    b. A full inhale pronouncing (H) "Hey",
    c. A full exhale pronouncing (V) "Vav",
    d. A full inhale pronouncing (H) "Hey",

4. With each letter turn 90 degrees

5. I would repeat these letters over and over again

6. Each letter is also representative of a face:

    a. Y – Lion
    b. H – Ox
    c. V – Eagle
    d. H - Man

Chp 2: Overview

Matthew 4:11-12 (AMP)

[11] *Then the devil departed from Him, and behold, **angels came and ministered** to Him.* [12] *Now when Jesus heard that John had been arrested and put in prison, He withdrew into Galilee.*

Hebrews 1:14 (AMP)

[14] *Are not the angels all ministering spirits (servants) sent out in the service [of God for the assistance] of those who are to inherit salvation?*

For this book, we will choose to have a Kingdom mentality, a renewed mind; by His invitation, we will think like our Abba Jehovah (Father God). Everything created has a purpose in His kingdoms.

With my team sports background and Yeshua's (Jesus') life, I believe one of the many types of resources of the Kingdom is on our team. We individually have calls & destinies but I feel we all need assistance from others in the Kingdom. The scriptures show that Yeshua needed assistance and he had access to resources (angels) in the Kingdom.

So acting on my beliefs, I used to have team meetings. I would go in the living room and talk strategies, goals, & objectives with the team. Some nights it was big things; some nights just discussing how the next should go. During those team meetings, I never saw anyone and did not hear any feedback. I talked, believed, and talked some more. I believe those months sitting and talking in the dark were getting ready for the kingdom. A few months later, I would not be disappointed. Angels were on my team (and your team).

So what's the big deal about angels?

Matthew 26:53 (AMP)
Do you suppose that I cannot appeal to My
Father, and He will immediately provide Me
(Yeshua) with more than twelve **legions**
[more than 80,000] **of angels**?

One day I was "appealing to My Father" and said, "How many
angels do I have access to?" I heard Him say, "You can have as
many as you can employ." It was tough getting my mind around
the word "employ". I was expecting to hear a unique number.
"Employ?" I didn't know that I needed to "pay" angels; what
currency do you use? After a few more natural consumer
thoughts, I realized that "employed" meant that the angels needed
to be assigned. Angels don't like to be passive; active is their
desired state.

How many angels will you employ?

Psalm 103:20
Bless the Lord, you **His** angels, you mighty
ones who [1]do **His** commandments,
hearkening to the [2] **voice of His word**.

1. Angels do Yahweh's commandments

2. If we will speak as him, we get to be His voice

Issues and Concepts

Colossians 2:18 (AMP)
[18] Let no one defraud you by acting as an umpire and declaring you unworthy and disqualifying you for the prize, insisting on self-abasement and worship of angels, taking his stand on visions [he claims] he has seen, vainly puffed up by his sensuous notions and inflated by his unspiritual thoughts and fleshly conceit,

We humans are so prone to worship stuff. So to be clear, **this book does NOT promote or endorse the worship of angels.** We don't worship but we need to know the other members of the team. Well some are members of your team; some are busy fulfilling their assignments, while others are waiting for us to mature.

There are other books and people that promote lies and false concepts such as:

1. The visible activity of angels has come to an end, because their mediating work is done;

2. Angels are a race of intelligent beings, of a higher order than man,

1 Corinthians 12:1 Young's Literal Translation (YLT)
"And concerning the spiritual things, brethren, I do not wish you to be ignorant;"

"Concept 1 people": sit in the "seat of the unbeliever" and actively hold to the concept that the ministry of angels has ended. Or they pre-determine that the ministry angels are NOT needed. Concerning spiritual things (the ministry of angels), it is not good to remain ignorant. Unbelief and ignorance are obstacles on your journey to being. Unbelief and ignorance extinguish the flames of life.

> ### Romans 12:2 (AMP)
> "*Do not be conformed to this world (this age), [fashioned after and adapted to its external, superficial customs], but be transformed (changed) by the [entire] renewal of your mind [by its new ideals and its new attitude], so that you may prove [for yourselves] what is the good and acceptable and perfect will of God, even the thing which is good and acceptable and perfect [**in His sight for you**].*"

"Concept 2 people" need to understand their intrinsic value. But is understanding possible with the brain (mind set, paradigms) that feeds on natural inputs? I heard once from a previous pastor that "reason was doubt in disguise". The first step in truly understanding our place in creation is to choose. We can choose "our sight" or "His sight". If we begin seeing others and seeing ourselves through His eyes – all we see will be transformed.

Though we currently spend most of our time in the natural world, it was NOT the original intent of YHVH to have us bound by physical laws and physical resources. These restrictions are the manifestation of frustrated creation. All of creation was impacted by Adam's fall from his first estate.

But now we have been given back access to the other laws and the other resources. Jesus is the door to the possibilities that the first Adam experience and much more. All things are possible to him who believes.

"… somewhere out there you have another father, and he sent you here for a reason. And even if it takes you the rest of your life, you owe it to yourself to find out what that reason is."

- Jonathan Kent ("Man of Steel 2013", the movie)

Process and Preparation

John 6:29 (AMP)
Jesus replied, This is the **work** (service) that
God asks of you: that you **believe** in the One
Whom He has sent [that you cleave to, trust,
rely on, and have faith in His Messenger].

When most people read or hear those words, "Process
and Preparation", their mind (like mine) translates that
into "how much work must I do". We need to really
change our thinking. We are called to live by Faith -
simply believe. Mentally, I have made this new creation
life hard, actually it seems impossible. If I would just
acknowledge these facts:

> I cannot **DO** enough;
> I cannot **WORK** hard enough;
> I cannot **PRAY** good enough or long enough;
> and
> I am not **SPIRITUAL** enough.

We just need to Know Him and Trust Him - It's all about
relationship.

> "No Relationship leads to No Life; No Life leads to No
> Fun in the Kingdom"

Romans 1:17 (NIV)
[17] For in the gospel the righteousness of God
is revealed—a righteousness that is by faith
from first to last, just as it is written: "The
righteous will live by faith."

After striving to make angel contact in 1975, our family moved to
Germany. I didn't stop believing but I pushed the "thought of
meeting my angel' to the back burner. I had this bad habit or

immature mindset of dealing with "failure". If I could NOT meet my goal, I would take the objective through three phases:

- Phase 1: Ignore the objective,
- Phase 2: Devalue the objective,
- Phase 3: Then enter the objective into my "reason cycle" (where I reason the point that not having the objective was to my benefit)

The reason cycle is very effective and it regularly leads to being normal and acceptable in religious circles. God (Yahweh) does not to like my reason cycles. He always intervenes in the lives of the ones HE loves.

He Loves You!

John 3:16 (AMP)
[16] For God so greatly loved *and* dearly prized the world that He [even] gave up His only begotten (unique) Son, so that whoever believes in (trusts in, clings to, relies on) Him shall not perish (come to destruction, be lost) but have eternal (everlasting) life.

Adonai (The Lord) loves us so much He continually provides opportunities for us to believe. On the topic of angels, it took me 36 years for me to believe. I am so glad that He is faithful and patient.

Philippians 1:6
And I **am** convinced *and* sure of this very thing, that **He Who began a good work** in you will continue until the day of Jesus Christ [right up to the time of His return], developing [that **good work**] *and* perfecting *and* bringing it to full completion in you.

In His goodness, He intervenes. Webster's definition of "Intervention" (I'm partial to 3b):

1: to occur, fall, or come between points of time or events

2: to enter or appear as an irrelevant or extraneous feature or circumstance

3a: to come in or between by way of hindrance or modification

3b: to interfere with the outcome or course especially of a condition or process (as to prevent harm or improve functioning)

4: to occur or lie between two things

5a: to become a third party to a legal proceeding begun by others for the protection of an alleged interest

5b: to interfere usually by force or threat of force in another nation's internal affairs especially to compel or prevent an action

Here are a few **interventions** that kept me on the journey that started in 1975 which led to actual contact in 2011.

While in college in the early '80, a friend of mine called me and said, "I've got something you need hear". He came to my dorm room and played a cassette. I expected to hear some exciting message but the tape just contained some singing with instrumental accompaniment from his mother's home bible study. I was not impressed with songs. Then, he mentioned that no one was playing instruments during the meeting and there were no musical instruments in his mom's house. I listened to the cassette again. There were also more voices on the tape than there were people in the house. Everyone's assumption was that angels were the source of the musical instruments and the additional voices that had an extreme vocal range. My friend made me a copy of the cassette. Now that I had fresh evidence, angels were back on my list.

This 2nd hand information was good but it did not lead to any contact; it only re-opened the case. I reviewed a few verses, prayed, but no one in my circles was talking about angels and I didn't see any.

19

A year or two later I had an unexplainable situation occur. I was driving two friends back to their college campus in flatlands of Kansas. It was dark and we were passing through many "one-stoplight-towns". As we were passing through one of these small towns, we were startled as we drove over some train tracks. So, the next set of tracks, I thought I would slow ease over these tracks. While I had my foot on the break and easing over the tracks, I turned my head to the left and I saw an oncoming train. This sighting caused the occupants of the car to scream like girls (no offense ladies). In the midst of the screams, somehow the car was stopped a few feet passed the tracks and the train cars were passing behind us. We screamed; the train continued. The train passed; we continued to scream. When the screaming ended, we sat in silence.

After the long silence, the guys began to thank me for saving their lives. I did not respond; I sat there trying to figure out what happened. I replayed the events in my mind. How did I accelerate across the tracks and stop so close to the train. My old car does not have that kind of power. If I moved my foot from the break to the gas, why did I return my foot back to the break? If I was moved by adrenalin, we should be still moving at a high speed down these small roads. We tossed around ideas, no one could figure it out; but we were all glad to be alive. It was late and we drove on. I think an angel moved our car.

Angelic Encounters

o **The Kingdom of God is not a trophy "to be put on your shelf".**
o **Angel encounters are not validations of mature spirituality.**
o **Angel encounters are not affirmations of a super, unique identity.**
o **Angel encounters are not events to be pursued.**
o **The Kingdom and angelic assistance are required to finish your race!**

Chp 3: Contact

During the 36 years, I tried everything: begging, repenting, caring, not caring, some crying, reading, conferences, cassette tapes, videos, CDs, more repenting, learning protocols, repenting for begging, relaxing, and...

I wasted a lot of time.

I just needed to be a believing believer who believes.

Mark 9:23 (AMP)
And Jesus said, [You say to Me], If You can do anything? [Why,] **all things can be (are possible) to him who believes!**

The "impossible" is possible for those new creations that believe. Seeing is NOT the evidence; the evidence is His promises!

John 12:37-38 (AMP)
[37] Even though He had done so many miracles before them (right before their eyes), yet they still did not trust in Him *and* failed to believe in Him—
[38] So that what Isaiah the prophet said was fulfilled: Lord, **who has believed our report** *and* our message? And to whom has the arm (the power) of the Lord been shown (unveiled and revealed)?

Believe His report NOT the report of your senses.

Free-At-Last

In April 2011, I was returning from my first Ian Clayton conference in Connecticut. On the drive back to Virginia, we listened to set of CDs called, "Understanding Angels" by Ian Clayton. I think the second CD got stuck in the CD player, so we listened to that message multiple times before we stopped. The group, which I attended the conference with, convinced me that it was better for us to stop at a friend's house for rest rather than to attend another east coast meeting. So, the caravan of two cars stopped at our friend's house in Pennsylvania.

I had heard a lot of new concepts and my brain was spinning so it was good to stop, process, and practice. I had learned, "Kingdom was so close to me all I need to do was to step-in (stand up and take a physical step forward) by faith." We had practiced this at the conference. I had practiced in the hotel room. And on the drive, I realized that since it was by faith, I did not need to physically stand up and take a step – I could "take a step into the Kingdom" even while driving. I had learned that I could be anywhere (even a friend's house) and step into the Kingdom. So I practiced while brushing my teeth and before bed.

Our host made us breakfast. The spread included a spinach omelet, oatmeal, turkey bacon, hot cocoa, and juice. I had to use my faith to eat the omelet. I was also trying to integrate "**John 6 communion**" into my day. So I used bacon and juice – I sat there stepped in, had communion, and while in the Kingdom I had a thought. The thought was, "somewhere in here I have a throne, I should find it..." I found it. I was pleased. I sat on it and I was very pleased. Meanwhile, my omelet was cooling to the sounds of DJ Caleb playing in background. I remained on the throne a bit longer. From this throne, I could see framed portraits. The portraits were very large; each had a name plate beneath them. I leaned forward to see if I could make out the images or the names; it was all fuzzy. As I focused on the name plates, I could make out letters but it was not English. It seemed to be in a language I hadn't learned yet. But somehow, I knew the portraits were of many different types of angels or spirit beings. The room was very large; it could have been some sort of "Hall of Honor". I thought it odd that this room would have portraits and my throne and portraits of angels? (I'm now learning that in those moments it is not time to try figure stuff out it's more important to "absorb it all".) I sat back on the throne.

When I sat back, my peripheral view saw something to my right. I turned my head and an angel was standing to the right of my throne. From the CD or the conference, I remembered: "**not to fear, to not panic**"; I belonged here. Then I calmly said,

"What is your name? "

"What is your purpose?"

My eyes were fixed on him. He seemed to be an angel of Might, very much a warrior. He was wearing tokens (souvenirs?) from past, present, & future victories. He had a heavy linked chain around his neck, some kind of crest/shield over his chest – I thought he looked very "savage". His name is "**Free-at-Last**". Not many words spoken but he knows intent & targets. He is mighty one sent to be my guardian, my keeper. I was impressed with his "physicality". So much to take in, I thought I should stop staring so I turned my head back to the center. I was not sure how to respond. I think, I was supposed to introduce myself but I was trying not to shout or do something stupid. Nothing had prepared me for the next steps. I resolved to just turn my head.

What a morning, I had found my throne and an angel. As I relished the moment, my peripheral view saw something else, something to my left.

Promise

I turned my head to the left, there stood another angel. She was taller than the first and a "she". She had long, jet black hair. She wore a garment that was made of multiple layers of a sheer fabric. The fabrics were different colors, shades of blue and purple. Was it shades or was it different textures? I again calmly said, "What is your name? What is your purpose?" Her name is "**Promise**". She was an angel of wisdom (counsel), I think from Michael's camp. She was assigned to make the promises of the King clearer to me. I believe her garments were symbolic of the various depth and dimensions of promises.

I found myself sitting again in front of my cold omelet, my host, and my two other friends. I devoured my food, including the omelet, and placed my plate, glasses, and utensils in the sink. I needed to write this "whatever just happened" in my journal. Avoiding conversation, holding to the memory, I went to my host's sun room.

I wrote frantically. As I was about to write the portion about Promise, I was interrupted. One my friends entered my sanctuary and said, "What are you doing?" With no eye contact I replied, "Writing". Then he said, "Did you know that your angel looks like a barbarian and has a chain around his neck and has a crest on his chest…" I looked up. I said, "What, you can see my angel – is that allowed?" My friend did not answer my question, turned, and walked out of the room. I returned to writing.

As I mentioned earlier, I was trying to integrate "John 6 communion" into the day. So later during lunch, I was having communion. As I brought the "body" to my mouth, I felt something lean over both of my shoulders. My two angels, Promise & Free-at-Last, leaned over my shoulders and watched. I thought this odd. I brought the "blood" to my mouth and they watched again. I wondered if this would happen every time I took communion. Why were they looking? It was distracting. It seems that they were attempting to comprehend the revelation I was engaging in. They do not take communion; Yeshua created them but did not give his body and blood for them. We have access to His life, power, and DNA. We are heirs; they are angels.

It seems that they had been assigned to me a long time ago – much earlier than today. They have not been very active; I think they were bored. I believe as I "be" and engage – they will engage and no longer be so bored.

I have great memories from that "rest stop" in Pennsylvania. But I had to return to my family and a job. I dropped my friends off in Washington DC and made it home to Virginia.

My Pennsylvania host had mentioned that he'd spent a longtime preparing the spiritual atmosphere of his home. His sun room was his prayer room. I wondered, "Could I have the same kind of spiritual encounters I had in Connecticut and Pennsylvania or do I need to wait until I can find/return to that special atmosphere?"

Or-ion and Holi-day

About a week or so after the meeting Free-at-Last, I had some free time. Actually, I made choice to take time to meditate. I had been stepping into the Kingdom as much as I could. I was regularly taking communion. All in all, I was enjoying and learning to enjoy my inheritance and doing my best to know the King and His Kingdoms.

At my (earth) father's house, I was meditating and engaging with the King. I thought, I would go outside to his backyard and add some fresh air to the equation. I got comfortable in a chair and returned to meditating. I opened my eyes. I was looking toward the neighbor's house. An object appeared as a bright ball of light in the distance. I thought it was a speck on my glasses. I wiped my glasses. I blinked. The "star" was still there. I focused on the bright little star and it seemed to come closer and closer. As it got closer it, it grew in size. The star became a ball. It must have been quite a distance away. As it came into range, what I thought was a ball took the form of a horse - a horse with wings. I continued to stare and then I saw a rider. The rider was swinging something over its head. They looked like bola which I'd seen when I had travelled to Argentina. The horse and rider landed on the deck about three feet from me. It looked like the horse bowed. The horse and rider stood tall, both a very bright white. I could not see a saddle. I expected him to dismount but he didn't. I asked, "What is your name? What is your purpose?" His name was, "**Or-ion**". I said, "Orion". He said "Ori-on". (I was pronouncing it in correctly. I thought this funny since I was not actually speaking. I learned that miss-pronouncing was not limited to the audio realm.) Anyway, Ori-on is a messenger angel, well actually "he was to bring me things from afar". I translated that as a "messenger angel". I'm not sure what it is that I needed from "afar" but I am ready and willing to receive. I thought it odd that he rode a flying horse. I had assumed all angels could fly. In fact, he can fly. I later found out that they met on a mission and were "joined" for their new assignment, me. He said there was an advantage to riding the horse rather than flying individually, but the reason was not comprehendible to me. We chatted briefly; then, they departed as fast as they arrived. After they left, I realized I was supposed to ask the horse its name. That thought was stranger than the encounter I just had. (Note: Later on Mother's Day, Sunday May 8th 2011, I found out that the horse could "speak" and its name was "**Holi-day**", pronounced "Holy Day".)

Colossus

I pondered the encounter, trying to recall the details, the feelings, the images, the conversation... Before I could finish processing, I saw something else. To my right something seemed to peek around the corner of the house. It was taller than the house. I was getting more comfortable with these encounters. The horse & rider were amazing – so a giant angel was "no big deal". So I quickly asked, "What is your name? What is your purpose? I was now much more familiar with the protocol. But, it seemed that this angel was not. He gave no response. I repeated, "What is your name? What is your purpose? It turned out that he was not an angel, but a creature. I was just glad to have him on my team. But He informed me he was not on my team. After a bit I did get his name, **Colossus**, but I didn't get or maybe I didn't hear his purpose. I was confused by his statement, "...not on your team".

26

I later found out none of them were on "my team". There was a team, it just was not mine. Colossus had a temporary assignment while Promise & Free-at-Last were long term. Don't ask me the difference between temporary and long term – all I know is it has nothing to do with the element called "time".

Reliant

It was a week of meeting the hosts. So one day I got a peek at another "Mighty One". I had just finished some time meditating and I was moving down the stairs. After meditating and engaging with the King, you kind of stay sensitive or maybe open to His realm.

> We need to remember and know that His realm is our realm too.

I went to sit in the TV room and I caught a glimpse of an angel. I followed the "protocols". His name is **Reliant**; he guards the perimeter, my flank. He teams with "Free at Last". Both are mighty warriors but servants to the Sons of God.
There is a principle of engaging the spirit realm; it is a simple principle: "believe and look".

Genesis 18:1-2 (AMP)
[1]Now the Lord appeared to Abraham by the oaks or terebinths of Mamre; as he sat at the door of his tent in the heat of the day,
[2] He lifted up his eyes and looked, and behold, three men stood at a little distance from him. He ran from the tent door to meet them and bowed himself to the ground

It's not clear how "sitting in the door of his tent in the heat of the day" was a prerequisite to the Lord's appearance. But he and we definitely have the ability to "look".

> **Believe and Look**

Igniter

During worship, he appeared "draped" in flames – a moving, living flame. It was quite the intro. I'm not sure how long he was in the room. Actually, there were several but only one engaged with me. The others were busy ministering to the people in congregation. I assume, they were seraphim but that's just because they were covered with fire. I did not ask what type he was but I did get a name, "**Igniter**".

> **Isaiah 6:2, 6 (AMP)**
> [2]*Above Him stood the* **seraphim***; each had six wings: with two covered his face, and with two covered his feet, and with two flew.*
> [6]*Then flew one of the* **seraphim** *to me, having a live coal in his hand which he had taken with tongs from off the altar;*

So based upon the biblical description and I didn't see any wings, definitely not six – I believe these beings enter the fire around the throne. The Lord inhabits the praises of His people so I believe during that night the Lord was present. I've noticed that where the Lord is present, some of His angels have a tendency to "hang around the throne".

> **Daniel 7:9 (AMP)**
> I kept looking until thrones were placed [for the assessors with the Judge], and the Ancient of Days took His seat, Whose garment was white as snow and the hair of His head like pure wool. His throne was like the fiery flame; its wheels were burning fire.

It seems that this class of angels enters the sound (worship) and then they ascend to other realms.

Chp 4: Some Protocols

1 Peter 3:22 (KJV)
[22] Who is gone into heaven, and is on the right hand of God; angels and authorities and powers being made subject unto him.

Angels move in our atmosphere just as a fish swims in water. I believe "Our atmosphere" is a combination of the [1]words we say and the [2]realms we "release".

There are classes/groups of different types of angels. Of these diverse groups many are assigned and others have non-earth missions. The assigned ones respond and interact with your words.

I believe there are at least two types of angels that are permanently assigned to your life and others have temporary assignments.

Angels have extreme respect for us; we are other spirit beings created by YHVH. Yet we are God's paramount creation; we are "God-class beings"; we are not small grasshoppers in our own eyes – "**we are God in their eyes**."

Some Interaction Guidance

- Give yourself permission to believe; belief is a requirement

- Relate to angels as a spiritual beings (one spiritual being to another type of spiritual being)

- You must acknowledge their existence (Hebrews 11:6) (Note: acknowledgment as they are; not based on: incorrect traditions, false speculations, Hollywood images, religious doctrines or demon doctrines)

- After acknowledging, you must be open to "relate": each has a role; each must know their "steps (Like a dance)

- Regular and growing interaction is needed for all 'healthy' relationships
- When they manifest, don't respond in fear (no screaming)
  a. Ask their name then
  b. Ask their purpose

Observations

- It seems that size, stature in the Kingdom is "relative"; relative to the situation, I believe size is a variable in different realms.

  - One day in an encounter, I appeared as a GIANT in front of my "normal" size angels and then moments later changed back to their size; Then back to HUGE size when I was making a declaration. Then I looked up to see the Lord very, very, very tall! Like His knees were in the clouds and we were unable to see beyond His waist... So I presume size is relative to the task or the need of the moment. My current theory is supported by the extra-biblical book, "Alice in Wonderland", by Lewis Carroll.

  - When in outer space. I was large enough to use my hands to actually place planets in their proper orbit. So I had the body and the ability to do what was necessary to be successful. (2 Corinthians 2:14a – "But thanks be to God, Who in Christ always leads us in triumph...")

- It is good to know and work with the assignment of the angel that is assigned to your local fellowship and or nation

- Angels like to be active

- There is time to listen and there is a time to command – the timing is refined in the relationship

Exercise

Hebrews 5:12-14 Young's Literal Translation (YLT)

[12] for even owing to be teachers, because of the time, again ye have need that one teach you what [are] the elements of the beginning of the oracles of God, and ye have become having need of milk, and not of strong food, [13] for every one who is **partaking** of milk [is] unskilled in the word of righteousness -- for he is an infant, [14] and of perfect men is the strong food, who because of the use are **having the senses exercised**, unto the discernment both of good and of evil.

From the Kingdom perspective: **seeing is participating**. I believe this concept is supported by some findings in the Quantum Physics arena, specifically the double-slit experiment. In that energy experiment, scientists watched a small portion of energy pass through two slits in a barrier, the energy behaved like a particle and went through one slit or the other. Yet when the experiment was repeated in the exact same controlled environment without a human watching (interacting) with the energy, it acted like a wave. Instead of selecting one of the two slits the energy went through both slits at the same time. At a minimum, this demonstrated that the behavior of energy changed based on a person's observation (interaction). It has been found that "when we observe (see) the object it's position is "influenced" by our engagement. I believe Yeshua supported this principle when he said, "I only do what I see my Father doing..."

John 5:19 (AMP)

[19] So Jesus answered them by saying, I assure you, most solemnly I tell you, the Son is able to do nothing of Himself (of His own accord); but He is able to do only what He sees the Father doing, for whatever the Father does is what the Son does in the same way [in His turn].

Every activity he did was out of Relationship - so as he observed (engaged thru seeing) his participation with His Father made all the difference in every realm... Another, way to say it - "if He didn't see it; He would not do it or If He did not See it; then it would not happen in the realms.

**Our observations
give permission for "things" to occur
in our realm of influence.**

Much has NOT occurred because we have NOT DARED to Look.

We have a responsibility to engage the Kingdom through Seeing.

QUESTION: If I SEE in the unseen realm; can it manifest in my realm?

Chp 5: Interactions

Every encounter in the Kingdom of our Father seems to give me permission or boldness to go a little further. I follow that New Testament principle: "to whom much has been given, much more will be given…" (Luke 19:26) or when the door is open – go explore the whole house….

> ## Luke 12:32 (AMP)
> Do not be seized with alarm *and* struck with fear, little flock, **for it is your Father's good pleasure to give you the kingdom**!

So after meeting several angels, I felt the door was open for more encounters. So with some perceived permission, I had a thought; maybe, I could explore the nations and meet the angel over each nation.

Choices build **STRONGHOLDS**

Choices build strongholds. These strongholds can be either good or bad. We know enough about building bad strongholds. The stronghold that has kept most of us in a "non-active state" is a stronghold called, "NATURAL". Every moment I utilize my natural senses (smell, touch, taste, hearing, & sight) I strengthen my bond to the earth and fortify NATURAL. It is time to be a spirit being and make the real realm paramount. It is time to invest in a Kingdom, son of God stronghold. The more that we turn from the natural and "turn aside" to the non-natural; we build a non-natural stronghold.

I believe the scripture is full of stories and even commands to help the process of building a godly stronghold. Here are 3 from the scriptures:

1. Meditate on the non-natural

    Joshua 1:8 (AMP)
    [8] *This Book of the Law shall not depart out of your mouth, but <u>you shall meditate</u> on it day and night, that you may observe and do according to all that is written in it. For then you shall make your way prosperous, and then you shall deal wisely and have good success.*

2. Engage in the non-natural

    Exodus 3:3 (AMP)
    [3] *And Moses said, I will now <u>turn aside</u> and see this great sight, why the bush is not burned.*

3. Dwell (imagine) the non-natural

    Psalm 91:1 (AMP)
    [1] *He who <u>dwells in the secret place</u> of the Most High shall remain stable and fixed under the shadow of the Almighty [Whose power no foe can withstand].*

Exploring nations

So before you ask, "No, I do not have a scripture for this activity and I do not know why God would allow this activity".

So my activity starts in my imagination. I would randomly choose a nation. In my imagination, travel to the nation. After landing, I would ask to engage with the Angel over the nation. We would chat. The discussion centered on the major issues over the nation and in what areas the angel needed assistance. It didn't seem that the conversation was that long. I know I didn't do the USA and the first nation I did was Australia. Part of my motivation is from my belief that I have a call to the nations. And I thought it would be good to "spy out the lands" before I travel to them. After each "Global Angelic Information Session", I would return to my room and then turn on my computer. With computer on I would seek to validate the information that I saw and heard. I would spend some time with Google and Wikipedia. Honestly, I was shocked when I returned from Australia and some of the info I retained was accurate.

Angels assigned to Churches

I believe every local assembly has at least one angel assigned to help fulfill the vision/mission of that group of people who come together on a frequent basis. I think it is to the benefit of the assembly to not just cooperate with angel but co-labor with them. So with this "new to me" belief, I started asking what the purpose of the angel was over the assemblies I attend or visit. The following are attended to encourage you to engage with the host over the assemblies that you attend. They are waiting!

> **1 Corinthians 12:1** (AMP)
> [1]Now about the spiritual gifts (the special endowments of supernatural energy), brethren, I do not want you to be misinformed.

Once during worship, in May 2011, I perceived a spirit-being in our midst. This being seemed to have keys around its neck. The keys were available to be distributed. I believe this being was the angel over this assembly. During some period of the service when the believers are 'accepting' (open to receive); keys are dropped into their open being. It seems the keys are then embedded in the believers. It seems the keys equip those believers for particular assignments that the key gives permission to enter into a place and the authority to enter and occupy.

During another service, in February 2012, I believe we had a "seraphim moment". I'm not sure if it was a vision or a corporate encounter. I saw fiery beings standing in front of the people and me. I had the sense that we "were not in the coal from the altar period' but in a new era. It seemed that if we were willing that these beings were able to take us by the hand and lead us into the fire. In His fire we are not just marked by the flame but we become ONE with the flame. When we live in Him & live in the flame, others will see the FIRE and not us.

In October 2013, we had a similar to the seraphim moment experience – except the fire began during the song – the fire beings were not visible but the "invitation into the FIRE" was the same.

The Angel over an assembly in Virginia

Our church was leaving our location in Washington DC. We were going to use a facility in Northern Virginia. It was closer to my home but I did wonder about the angelic dynamic. The facility was already the home a congregation that used the site for a school during the weekday and ministry services on Sunday. Our congregation would use the facility on Saturday eve. Before we actually moved, the other group invited some of the members to visit and learn the history of our future gathering site.

During our visit, I believe I saw the angel assigned to the site and heard the word "REFUGE". I believe the angel is an angel of refuge or His name is "Refuge". I believe his assignment was to make the place (the 18 acres) and the people - a place of refuge and a people of refuge. As I continued to focus, I could see him swinging something over his head - as he swung he was creating a swirling, circular column - similar to a tornado except the whole at top and bottom were the same diameter. In the center of this swirling column, there was a refuge of peace and tranquility. The angel had made "atmospheres" for the land and for the people. It seemed to me that during portions of the sites history, the people who gathered here for "church"; seemed to have miss-interpreted the purpose of this "divine refuge". It seems that the people thought the winds were a sign of 'separation' - created to keep people from the church and to isolate the people away from the world. It seems that people perceived the place to be "a fortress of solitude for a chosen people." I believe the atmosphere created by the angel was to be a model to be duplicated by the members of the fellowship. Each member was to be an atmosphere of Peace & Presence in a world of turmoil. When assembled, they were to expand the boundaries of this "peace" beyond the 18 acres - to expand the borders of the swirling, circular column to encapsulate Northern Virginia so the land and the people would continually experience the peace of the Lord. The "refuge" was created for the MANY not the few!"

Angel over an assembly in Maryland

I was visiting a friend's congregation. I arrived early and was invited to play with the worship team on stage. I'm not very comfortable playing on stage or in front of people but I do enjoy playing my djembe. Anyway, when playing a new song I usually take my rhythm clues from the lead singer, lead guitar, bass guitar, or the kit drummer (in that order). So as I was looking, I saw someone to my right, across the stage, behind the bass player. The person did not have an instrument and it seemed to be "peeking" from behind the stage curtains. I ignored the person because I was losing the beat. I got the beat and closed my eyes to enjoy the worship. After a few minutes, I opened my eyes and looked out into the audience. They seemed to be engaged as well.

About half though the worship, I saw that person peeking again from behind the curtains. I had visited this Maryland fellowship many times but I didn't recognize the person. So, I looked again. It was an angel but it (he) looked like a blond haired young man wearing blue jeans. Then, I heard him say, "I have been here for some time and I would like to be active with this group". What I believe was also in the message was that the fellowship's ignorance of the kingdom resource would limit their influence in the territory.

Follow-on

This "follow-on" section is to remind you that your interaction with the angelic is relationship based – or otherwise stated – "they are committed to their missions; it is an ongoing interaction with the resources of our King!"

> **Luke 12:32 (AMP)**
> Do not be seized with alarm *and* struck with fear, little flock, for it is your Father's good **pleasure** to give you the **kingdom**!

> **Romans 8:32 (AMP)**
> He who did not withhold or spare [even] His own Son but gave Him up for us all, will He not also with Him freely and graciously give us all [other] things?

"Stop being surprised that Our Good Father is so lavish with His resources. He is holding nothing back; He has made EVERYTHING AVAILABLE! He has fully equipped us to be successful on earth and where ever we have missions!"

The conversations that are below are just conversations. If you view yourself as a "mere human" and not as special, new creation in Christ Jesus that has been made righteous and qualified... then you think the below conversations are at worst a form of idolatry (angel worship) or best a product of an over active imagination. Now, the below conversations to not supersede my conversations with my Heavenly Father; just like a conversation between you and I would not supersede your relationship with Abba.

PROMISE

(April 2011) In a conversation on Easter, I was curious about if there was a relationship between the angelic and the seven spirits of God. So, I asked. Promise mentioned that she not only knows the spirit of Wisdom but she (Promise) is the one who introduced me and led me to her (Wisdom). I was a bit surprised by her statement. It was very insightful but now I need to decide if I needed to create a 4th edition to my other book, *Introduction to the Seven Spirits of God* (Amazon). Not that I doubted her but I asked the other angels if they also knew the spirit of Wisdom and they did.

(December 2013) A friend not knowing what I was writing sent me the following excerpt from the extra-biblical Book of Enoch:

> **Enoch 42: 1-2**
> [1]*Wisdom did not find a place where she might dwell; so her dwelling was in the heaven.*
> [2]*Wisdom went forth to dwell among the sons of men, but she did not find a dwelling.*
> *Wisdom returned to her place, and sat down her seat among the angels.*

(Jan 2012) During a visit of a friend's assembly in Washington DC, Promise appeared in the middle of the worship service. I heard and saw her sing over us. She was singing what we were singing to the Father. She sang (and pointed), "You are good, you are good, and your love endures forever". I did not ask anyone else if they saw her.   On this Sunday, it was a teenager's birthday. It is the custom of this congregation to sing "Happy Birthday (English & Spanish) and to bless them with a prophetic word or scripture. Today, I repeated the activity that I saw the angel, Promise do. I sang the same song over the young lady. My voice is not the best but I more focused on engaging with my Father's business than my vocal prowess. I sang over the teenager for 16th birthday.

For more detail, you can research the accounts of different people who minister with "angelic support" (see James Mahoney, Paul Keith Davis, Steven Brooks, Judith MacNutt, and others…)

Free-at-last

I asked Free-at-Last if He knew the spirit of Wisdom. He also knew her. He said, "I received and receive strength from her." He went on to say, "Many of my victories were due to her wisdom and insights."

Later, Free-At-Last told me he was the one that appeared in my basement those many years ago (1975, read *Introduction, pg. 5*). I did wonder why he waited so long to tell me. He said, "He wondered why I waited so long to hear."

Ori-on & Holi-day

My wife is an equestrian and she has a horse named Al. I love my wife and you spend time with people you love. So on this day, I went with her to the stable. She went to prepare her horse to ride and I sat down to read a book. It was a beautiful day. She came out on her horse; they looked good together. I missed a great photo opportunity. She and Al walked towards the circle arena. I thought this was going to be a good day for a read until… To my surprise Holi-day and Ori-on appeared to my right. This was new, I mean, I wasn't meditating; I wasn't engaging with the King; and my eyes were open and I was at a horse stable. I turned toward the two and my first thought was, "Can the horses see you?" Holi-day said, "Yes and Al is not his real name…" I didn't know which was stranger: 'talking to these two in public' or 'the fact that my wife's horse has a different name'? Before I could ponder further, I heard screams. I turned to see Al galloping and my wife out of control. The horse was running toward the stable; the stable owner was screaming and I was watching hoping my wife would hold on. My wife decided to let go and fall off and the horse ran free. I dropped my book and ran to my wife. The stable owner yelled for someone to grab the horse. I saw my wife land; she just missed the arena bars but landed hard on the ground. Soon horse and rider were reunited. Just like in the movies, she got back in the saddle; I returned to my seat.

41

My wife needed to show who was boss and I needed to understand. I was not sure how this bad could happen on "my watch". I didn't think anything bad could happen with me being present – I thought I was walking in "dominion". I turned to my two angels for clarity or an explanation. I said, "Did one or both of you spook the horse? And how come you guys didn't do anything to help the situation?" They said, "Look again". I turned my head back to the scene and in my mind or imagination I saw the scene again but this time a bit slower: "Some black came out the ground, Al was spooked, reared up, and began to run. I saw my wife make the decision to fall off and then saw Ori-on ease her to the ground and not into the metal bars of the round arena. Before Al could run too far, Holi-day stopped his progress allowing the stable hand to not have to run after Al. "I thought, "Wow, that replay was much different from the 'live' scene". I felt better that they were involved but what was that "black thing" that came up from the ground. I replayed the scene over and over again in my mind's eye. Needless to say, I didn't read much that day.

I now understood what occurred, but I had a new dilemma – should I tell my wife what happened. I decided not to tell her unless she asked me what I saw. I think Ori-on suggested that strategy. Anyway, she finished her ride, cleaned the horse, put him up, and we walked together to the car. We lived almost 30 minutes away and she began to tell me her version of the day's events and what she needed to convey to the horse after the fall. I listened intently waiting for my opportunity to tell her what I saw and what Ori-on and Holi-day did.

She finally said the magic words, "So what did you see?" This was not the first time she had heard about Ori-on & Holiday. But this was the first time for hear what I saw – which was very different from what she experienced. To my amazement, she believed me. She didn't believe me because I told her; she believed me because of what Holi-day said. Remember, I had said, "Can they see you" and they said, "Yes". Then, Holiday said, "Yes and Al is not his real name" I said, "What's his real name?" Holi-day said, "He does not want you to know. " Holiday said, "Al likes the fact that my wife likes calling me Al and he likes her to be happy – so he did not want to upset her by having her think that 'all this time' she had been calling him the wrong name." When he originally said that, I thought that was "stupid" but it ended up being the thing that made the whole thing believable to my wife.

I'm not sure that you believe but that is fine. You should have more questions like:

- Where was my wife's angel(s)?
- Where did the black thing go?
- How come I didn't see everything in the territory?

> **Proverbs 25:2 (AMP)**
> "It is the **glory** of God to conceal a thing, but the **glory** of **king**s is to **search** out a thing."

Questions are good.

They allow you to be a king and keep you on the journey.

Leaves
(Nov 2012) In the fall, the tree in our front yard dumps its leaves on the front yard. I think the multi-colored blanket on the front lawn makes it look better than the grass. My wife does not share the same perspective. With the falling of the leaves, the rake requests to rake. I respond, "Why would I rake now and tree still has leaves". I was granted a temporary reprieve. My Monday commute from work took me home to be greeted with a rake and an announcement, "The tree is free from leaves". I submitted, changed clothes, and began the chore. I thought about listening to an mp3 while raking but my ear buds may not cooperate with

this physical activity. So I raked and bagged leaves without a sound track.

Matthew 28:20 (AMP)
"… I am with you all the days (perpetually, uniformly, and on every occasion)…"

Without the audio distractions, I was free to ponder. So I thought, "Why can't my angels just lend a hand and help me rake & bag these leaves?" This was not too odd of a thought, since angels do minister to the heirs of salvation… My pondering led me acknowledge my angels (Reliant, Ori-on, Holi-day...) Plus, I felt my angelic group were present watching me rake.

Live in the reality that He is with you in every occasion!

As I was raking in "this reality", I heard, "You wouldn't want them to rake, because they are 'specialist' - good at whatever they do; they do well and they are not 'multi-taskers'". From that statement, I understand "an angel could guard me or rake for me but not both."
I raked and thought about "my specialists". After a few bags, I remembered a message about a monk in 740 A.D. who knew the names of over a hundred angels. I thought, "How did that monk talk with over a hundred angels?" It's a challenge to balance communicating with just a few angels. I heard two things:

> 1. "Like a radio, you broadcast messages and many are listening;
> 2. "Spiritual beings are drawn to shouting messages"

I will let you ponder on those statements and if you draw near to Abba, He may reveal to you what those statements may mean to you. Note: I finished the evening with 9 large bags of leaves.

Planet with 3 suns
There are good and bad things on Face Book. I was invited to a late night Face Book event, "Third Heaven Experiences, Travelling

in the Spirit and Other Stuff" (Aug 2013); I accepted. The event was facilitated via an audio Skype session. The teacher led us through several 'activations'. One of the activations, he asked us to go through a door. I closed my eyes and went through a door in the spirit realm. On the other side of the door, I came to a place that had 3 suns in the sky. I assumed it was some planet in some galaxy, somewhere. I heard, "You are at an angel training ground". I didn't know and I've never read about an 'angel training ground'.

Colossians 1:26 (AMP)
"The mystery of which was hidden for ages and generations [from angels and men], but is now revealed to His holy people (the saints),"

The above scripture alludes to the point that people and angels don't know everything – some things are yet to be revealed and are being revealed. So I guess this was a place that "mysteries" were being revealed to angels and the word of God is their standard. It seemed that:

- They must not lean upon their own (angelic) understanding [see Proverbs 3: 4,5]
- This was a place to be trained to deal with human's bodies and souls
- This was a place to learn to deal with 'sowers'. It seems that angels do not sow but they reap [see Matthew 13:41].

It was good to know that the angels, who are sent to minister, are trained & qualified for ministry. I also learned from this encounter that:

- Angels minister without a time limit to Abba's creations, called humans
- The seven spirits of God train within a time limit to Abba's creations, called humans

Angels in the Courtroom

Revelation 12:10-11a (AMP)

[10]Then I heard a strong (loud) voice in heaven, saying, Now it has come--the salvation and the power and the kingdom (the dominion, the reign) of our God, and the power (the sovereignty, the authority) of His Christ (the Messiah); for the accuser of our brethren, he who keeps bringing before our God charges against them day and night, has been cast out! [11]And they have overcome (conquered) him by means of the blood of the

> The accuser can go to court frequently unannounced to do his job of accusation; therefore, it is wise to go to the courts often!

Lesson: I have learned that you can summon the accuser but he will rarely summon you when he is accusing you before the Judge. Your case and testimony contains the potential to bring the victory.

[September 2013] On this morning while putting in contacts in my peripheral vision to my left, I saw something. I turned and saw a tiny spider suspended in midair, a little lower than my left shoulder. I was not shocked but more surprised. How did I become aware or alerted or perceived the presence of the spider?

After I crushed the spider, I kept thinking of how and why I saw the spider. I had no thoughts about killing the spider. Then I had this idea, "the spider has something to do with the 'accuser of the brethren' and a reminder for me to go to the courts." But, I'm late so I don't act on my idea.

A few hours later during a live worship event, I thought I would step in and check into what was going on in the courts. Before entering the court, I thought I would get some counsel. I had some questions: "Did the enemy summon me? I didn't think that possible - was court in session?" I had some counsel and received some

46

peace. Then, I enter in the midst of the accuser spewing accusations against me. I interrupted. I could see the accuser was surprised at my presence. I felt the court was relieved at my arrival.

I had learned to agree with my accuser quickly [Matthew 5:25]; therefore, I agreed with my accuser. The accuser was right - I had been acting independently. Then, I began my case with promises & my testimony: "I no longer live, I am not my own... We are one; Since He is for me....)

Case closed; I won.

What was I to do with an accuser who has 24/7 access to the courts?

What if I'm not there when, he is spewing?

I had a thought maybe I could be notified - I then thought of my angel, Promise.

In the scope of ministry of angels assigned to me (us) - could I have (assign) an angel to the courtroom - monitoring the court night and day?

I believe yes.

Chp 6: New Testament References

An angel appears three times in dreams to Joseph (Matthew 1:20; 2:13, 19).

The angel Gabriel appears to Zacharias, and then to Mary (Luke 1).

An angel announces to the shepherds the birth of Jesus, and is joined by a "multitude of the heavenly host," (Luke 2:8).

When Jesus' temptation was over, angels appear to Him to strengthen Him (Matthew 4:11).

When Jesus was in the agony at Gethsemane, angels appear again to strengthen Him (Luke 22:43).

An angel came down to stir the pool (John 5:4).

An angel descends to roll away the stone from the tomb of Jesus (Matthew 28:2);

Angels are seen there by certain women (Luke 24:23);

Two angels were seen by Mary Magdalene (John 20:12).

An angel releases the apostles from prison, (Acts 5:19)

An angel directs Philip (Acts 8:26).

An angel appears to Cornelius in a vision (Acts 10:3).

An angel frees Peter from prison (Acts 12:7).

An angel strikes Herod (Acts 12:23).

An angel appears to Paul in a dream (Acts 27:23, 24).

According to our Lord angels describe a trait of the resurrected life – no marriage (Matthew 22:30);

Twelve legions (80,000) of angels could have been summoned to the aid of our Lord, had He so desired (Matthew 26:53);

Angels will accompany Him at the Second Coming (Matthew 25:31)

Angels will separate the righteous from the wicked and be very active in the last days (Matthew 13:41, 49).

Angels rejoice when people repent (Luke 15:10);

Angels are active on behalf of children (Matthew 18:10).

Some angels will be judged by the saints (1 Corinthians 6:3).

There is absolutely NO Benefit in the worship of angels (Colossians 2:18).

Angels are described as ministering spirits engaged in the service of the saints. (Hebrews 1:14)

Jesus has supremacy over all created spiritual beings (1 Peter 3:22).

Also the book of Zechariah is a great handbook on the interactions of angels with a "non-mere man". It is possible the Book of Enoch may provide some insights but that was Enoch dealing with "fallen" angels.

There are people who right now have angelic encounters and that is the high point of their life; they make the encounter their identity. I know when I pursued my angel in the beginning; it led to no encounter & frustration. When I was pursuing maturity in YHVH - I met them.

Conclusion

Well you've met my angels and hopefully learned something new to help you in your journey. It's my opinion that we cannot fulfill our destiny without the resources that our Heavenly Father has made available.

Hebrews 12:21-25 (AMP)

[21] In fact, so awful *and* terrifying was the [phenomenal] sight that Moses said, I am terrified (aghast and trembling with fear).

[22] But rather, you have come to Mount Zion, even to the city of the living God, the heavenly Jerusalem, **and to countless multitudes of angels** in festal gathering,

[23] And to the church (assembly) of the Firstborn who are registered [as citizens] in heaven, and to the God Who is Judge of all, and to the spirits of the righteous (the redeemed in heaven) who have been made perfect,

[24] And to Jesus, the Mediator (Go-between, Agent) of a new covenant, and to the sprinkled blood which speaks [of mercy], a better *and* nobler *and* more gracious message than the blood of Abel [which cried out for vengeance].

[25] So see to it that you do not reject Him *or* refuse to listen to *and* heed Him Who is speaking [to you now]. For if they [the Israelites] did not escape when they refused to listen *and* heed Him Who warned *and* divinely instructed them [here] on earth [revealing with heavenly warnings His will], **how much less shall we escape if we reject *and* turn our backs on Him Who cautions *and* admonishes us from heaven**?

As we can see in verse 25, the Israelites did not take advantage of believing and relying on the provided resources – they did not finish their journey. We will learn from their example and not end as they did.

Some of you are saying that you have not met an angel yet? I disagree; I believe you just did not recognize your angel encounter. I know this from experience and from: Hebrews 13:2(NIV) – *"Do not forget to show hospitality to strangers, for by so doing some people have shown hospitality to angels without knowing it."*

I hope you have been encouraged to seek first the Kingdom which Abba has delighted in giving us. I hope you are eager to be active in spiritual things since you are a spiritual being like your heavenly Father

---

Seeing angels is optional;
fulfilling **Your Destiny** is mandatory and
I believe angelic assistance is necessary.

"I am as you saw me before you created me;
I am doing all that you saw me do.
I am BEING all you designed me to BE.
I rest and STRIVE NOT because,
You are my source!
I am One with You."

-New Mystic

Contact me on Facebook under the name: *New Mystic or*

Send email to 1newmystic@gmail.com

www.newmystic.net

55105767R10030

Made in the USA
Charleston, SC
20 April 2016